2 Great Ayton B

A fairly level circu[lar walk over a]n area of high moorland.
Fine views. Poss[ibly muddy]. 3¾ miles/6km;
Total Height Cli[mb: ...]

S. Sheet OL26

To reach the sta[rt, follow]
the instructions [given]
about the midd[le of ...]
the road to reach the s[ignposted]
posted paths. Ignore the Cleve[land]
Way (straight on: the return route) and
take the bridleway to the left.

The clear path swings left and
climbs. After a short distance it jinks
to the left and there is a split. Keep
right, on the clearer path. This runs
parallel to the wood (and Cleveland
Way) to the left, before contouring
round to the right, around the head of
a valley, to reach the gate at the end
of a public road.

Do not go through the gate but
head back-left on a clear, signposted
bridleway. After ½ mile/0.8km you
pass a brick hut then descend to the
edge of a conifer forest (the Cleveland Way cuts off to the right just
before you reach it). Go through a
gate on the edge of the trees. At the
junction beyond go left (bridleway),
along the edge of the trees with a
fence to your left.

Continue like this (ignoring a path
marked by a black arrow pointing
right, into the trees) until the edge of
the wood heads off to the right. Continue by the trees for a further 40m
to reach a junction marked by a post.
Go left here (blue arrow), passing
through a pedestrian gate and following a clear path across the moorland.

This leads you to a junction by
another wood. If you go through the
gate in front of you you will join the
Roseberry Topping path (*see* Walk 1).
For this route, however, turn left, with
a wall to your right and trees beyond
that. Various paths head off to the left
along the way, but stick by the wall
and you will return to the start.

3 Cook Monument _____B

A brief climb to a monument and viewpoint, a descent – steep in places – through woodland and a return by quiet public road. Possible links with Walks 1 & 2. **Length: 3 miles/5km; Height Climbed: 660ft/200m.**

O.S. Sheet OL26

Great Ayton is 3 miles south of Guisborough on the A173. From the High St, follow the signs for the station (Station Rd). The road climbs out of the village. At its highest point, just beyond a cattle grid, there is a large car park to the right.

Walk back to the cattle grid and turn left just before it (sign: Cleveland Way) on a clear track. You pass through a gate and a path heads off to the right: ignore this and keep straight on, into the conifer wood. After ½ mile/0.8km the track leaves the trees and crosses moorland to the Cook Monument (the great explorer spent his youth in Great Ayton). Turn right from the monument. The path descends then swings right to reach two gateposts in a tumbledown wall.

Beyond the gateposts you are on a clear, straight path with a broken down wall to your left. At the far corner of the wall a yellow arrow points ahead-left, down and across the slope.

The path enters a conifer wood and continues to descend, increasingly steeply. Cross a path running across the slope and continue to the gate at the bottom of the wood. Walk on a short distance beyond this with a wall to your right. When this turns right the path follows it.

Follow the wall until it ends, then continue with fences to either side. The path runs by a small wood then continues, eventually joining the end of a metalled road (ignore the track off to the left) and continuing, between houses, to a road junction.

Turn right onto Dikes Lane and follow it out of the houses. The road is quiet but also narrow. Listen out for traffic.

After ½ mile/0.8km the road passes a telephone box and there is a junction. Go right, along the back of Gribdale Terrace. At the end of the houses, when the road swings left, keep straight on. Edge right, to cross a stile into a field, then continue in the same direction. Climb to a stile then continue, with a fence to your left, back to the start.

Introduction

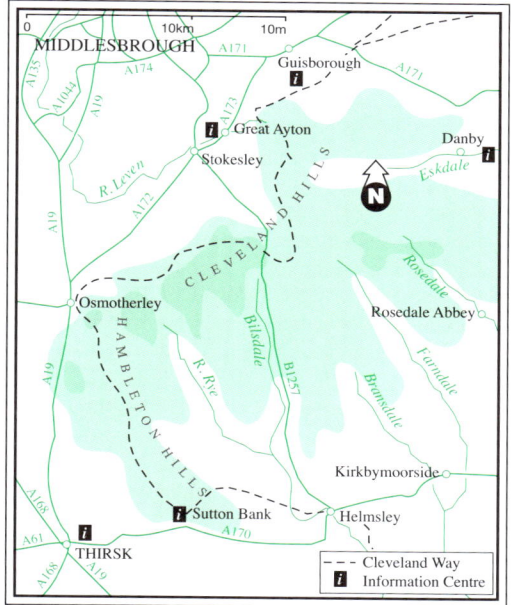

The North York Moors is an area of moorland intersected by narrow dales, butted up against the coast in the north-eastern corner of Yorkshire. The area covered measures approximately 30 miles from north to south and 40 miles from west to east. The population is low – and largely confined to villages and towns around the edge of the area. Eskdale, the largest of the dales, runs east to west across the northern part of the area; all other significant dales run approximately north to south. The area became a national park in 1952.

This series covers the North York Moors in two guides, dividing the Moors into eastern and western areas. This guide covers the western area, including walks along the dramatic northern and western edges of the Moors and in and around the narrow dales as far east as the villages of Danby (in the north) and Rosedale Abbey (in the south).

Disused Kilns (Walk 24)

There are no major towns in this area. The city of Middlesbrough sits just to the north, and all other towns of any size are arranged around the edge of the Moors: Guisborough to the north, then Great Ayton and Stokesley; Osmotherley *(Walks 12,13)* and Thirsk to the west; Helmsley *(16)* and Kirkbymoorside along the A170 to the south. The major roads likewise follow the edge of the hills – with the exception of the B1257, linking Stokesley and Helmsley along Bilsdale.

The majority of the walks in this guide are over moorland, following paths and tracks which are typically rough but clear. There are some steep climbs, but there are no high hills. The highest point in the North York Moors is Round Hill (1489ft/454m) *(9)*, but as it name might suggest it is not a dramatic crag. The most distinctive hill in the area is Roseberry Topping *(1)*: a miniature Matterhorn on the northern edge of the Moors. In the guide, this walk is linked to two others *(2,3)*, leading south as far as the prominent monument to Captain James Cook (brought up on a farm near Great Ayton).

South of these walks are three further paths following the Cleveland Way along the edge of the Moors: Ingleby Bank *(7)*, Round Hill and The Wain Stones *(8)* – the latter making a short climb to a broken tor. From all these walks there are fine views over the low land to the north and west.

To the east is the head of Eskdale. The bulk of the dale is covered by the companion volume (*Walks North York Moors: Eastern Area*), but this guide includes two walks from the little village of Danby *(5,6)* – one of them a link with the village of Commondale – and a fine moorland circuit around the Baysdale Beck *(4)*.

South of Eskdale the moorland rises to a watershed, beyond which three long, narrow dales – Rosedale, Farndale and Bransdale – empty southwards between long, heathery ridges. Relics of the 19th-century mining industry lend an incongruous backdrop to the moorland walks above Rosedale and the head of Farndale *(21,23,24)*. Farndale itself is better known for it daffodils *(18)*, though there are also fine walks along the ridge to the west *(19,20)*.

Sutton Bank (Walk 14)

The fine old village of Helmsley, with its ruined castle, sits by the River Rye on the edge of the hills. There is a pleasant lineal walk leading west from here, through farmland and woodland, to the village of Rievaulx and its splendid ruined abbey *(16)*, plus a further walk up the valley beyond *(17)*. Further up Ryedale are the forestry/moorland walk at Newgate Bank *(10)* and the long moorland circuit over Hawnby Moor *(11)*.

In the far south-west corner of the North York Moors is the steep escarpment on the edge of the Hambleton Hills. The National Park Information Centre at Sutton Bank sits at the point where the A170 begins to descend the bank. The guide contains two walks from the centre: north to Gormire Lake *(14)* and south to the white horse cut into the hill above Kilburn *(15)*.

The Cleveland Way

The map at the start of this section shows the line of the Cleveland Way, and as a number of the walks in the guide make use of this path it is worth explaining what it is.

The Cleveland Way is a long distance path, opened in 1969. In total, it runs 110 miles/176km around the moors and along the coast. The western end of the Way is at Helmsley. From there it runs west then north-east along the edge of the moors before joining the coast at Saltburn and heading south-east to reach Filey.

The route can be walked in either direction and will take approximately nine days of steady walking to complete. The paths are generally good and the signage clear. The routes in this guide which make use of the Cleveland Way are *Walks 1,2,3,7,8,9,13,14,15* and *16*.

Cleveland Way Logo

1 Roseberry Topping ─────────────────────── B

*A short, steep, popular climb to the top of a distinctive hill. Fine views. Possible links with walks 2 and 3. Length: **2½ miles/4km**; Height Climbed: **220ft/72m**.*

O.S. Sheet OL26

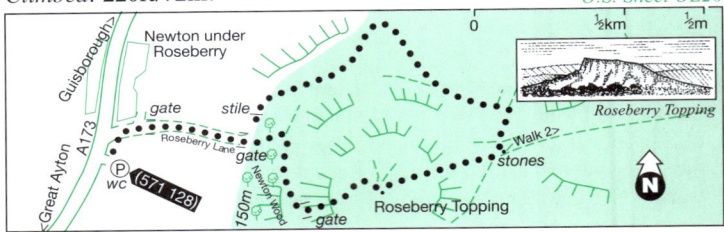

Start this walk from the little village of Newton under Roseberry, 2 miles south of Guisborough on the A173. Park in the car park on the southern edge of the village.

Walk to the north end of the car park (ie, towards the village) and turn right up a metalled road (sign: bridleway). When the tarmac road turns left keep straight on, passing through a gate and following a clear, rough track (Roseberry Lane) up to a gate on the edge of Newton Wood.

Beyond the gate there are a number of paths: go straight ahead. The path climbs the first slope, swings left, then continues to the top of the wood. The path leaves the trees and splits. Take the clearer, right-hand path, climbing up and across the slope on the upper edge of the wood. After a short way it swings left, through a gate in a fence, and climbs to the top of the hill over open ground.

Having enjoyed the fine view head left along the summit ridge then follow the clear path down to the saddle between Roseberry Topping and Newton Moor. At the lowest point, where a path heads off to the right, you have a choice. To link with Walk 2, keep straight on; to complete this circuit, go left. (Two or three paths head left at this point. Look for a pile of stones just opposite the start of the path to the right and take the clear path to the left of the stones.)

After a short distance paths cut off to right and left. Ignore these. After 200m you reach a junction marked by a post. Go left here (blue arrow).

The rough path descends through bracken and scattered trees. At the lowest point there is a split. Go right (yellow arrow) and follow a rough path around the end of a ridge then back towards Newton Wood, now with a fence to the right and fields beyond that. When the path forks keep left (to avoid a muddy patch) and keep straight on, crossing a stile on the edge of the trees then continuing straight on to reach the top of Roseberry Lane.

4 Baysdale B

A fine loop through moorland and farmland on clear paths and a quiet public road. Good views over the moors. **Length: 5 miles/8km**; **Total Height Climbed: 490ft/150m**.

O.S. Sheet OL26

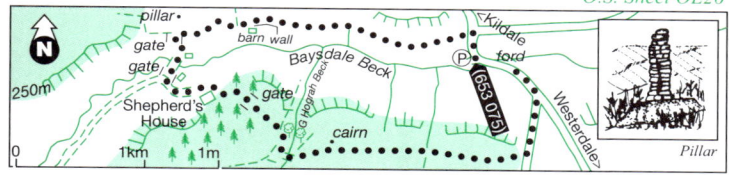

Pillar

Kildale is a small village 3½ miles (by road) south-east of Great Ayton. Just over a mile east of Kildale there is a four-way junction. Turn right here (Westerdale) and follow the narrow road for a little over 2 miles to reach a car park by the ford over Baysdale Beck.

Walk back up the road (ie. leave the car park and turn left), climbing to the point where a road heads off to the right and there is a sign for a bridleway to the left. Go left.

The clear track runs along the moorland slope for a mile/1.6km before being joined by a wall around fields to the left. Just past a barn a bridleway heads off to the right. Ignore this and continue by the wall until, level with a stone pillar up to your right, there is a gate in the wall.

Go through the gate and walk straight down the field beyond. Below a band of gorse the route ahead becomes visible: passing just to the right of a disused shed then swinging right to reach a bridge over Baysdale Beck; passing to the right of a barn, just beyond, to join a track (gate); then turning left up this track to reach a house (Shepherd's House) on the edge of a conifer plantation.

Edge left just before the house to reach a gate in a wall, beyond which a clear track climbs through a band of woodland to reach a gate on the edge of the moor. Beyond the gate, take the rough track which starts by hugging the trees to the right then heads off across the moor. In a short distance you join a fence around a wooded valley. Walk on a short way to reach a cairn by the track, level with a wooden gate in the fence to your left.

Do not go through the gate. Instead, follow a faint path which runs by the fence. When the fence goes hard left the path descends to a fine old stone bridge over Great Hograh Beck. Cross this.

Beyond the beck there are two or three paths running through the heather. Take the one which will lead you just to the right of the cairn (Alan Clegg) visible on the horizon. Beyond the cairn the path is clearer; running straight for ¾ mile/1.2km to join the public road. Turn left to return to the start.

5 Danby _____ B

A short circuit above a small village, following a sequence of rough paths and tracks through farmland, woodland and moorland. Length: **2½ miles/4km**; *Height Climbed:* **260ft/80m**.

O.S. Sheet OL27

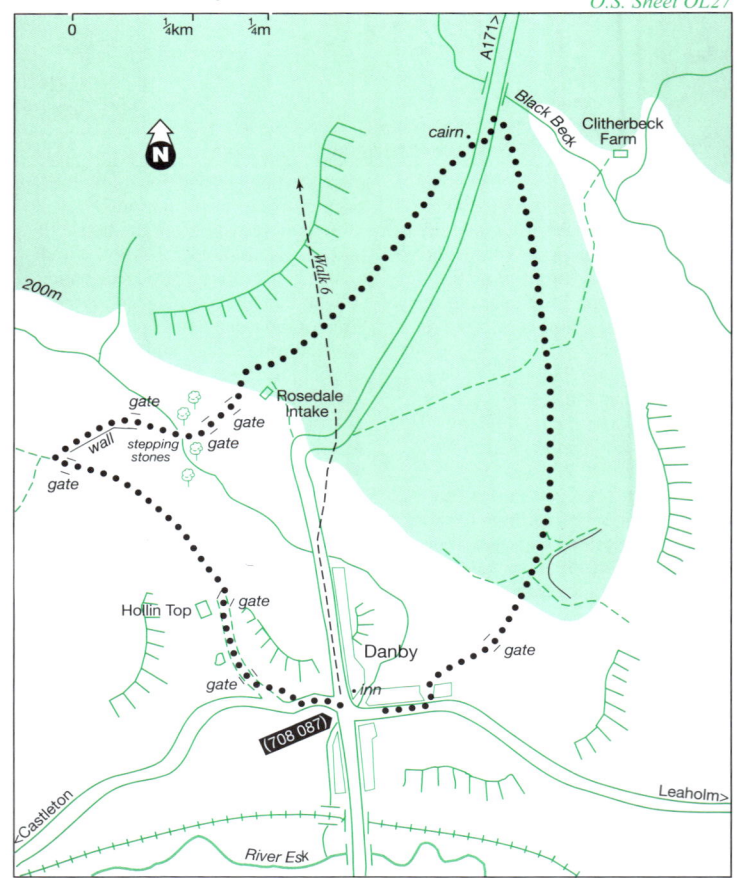

Danby is a small village in the upper Esk Valley. To reach it, drive west from Whitby on the A171 for about 12 miles then turn left (ie, south) on the road signposted for the village.

Park in the village and walk to the central crossroads, by the Duke of Wellington Inn. Walk west from here, on the road to Castleton. Pass the sign on the edge of the village for the end of the speed limit. A few metres beyond there is a sign for a footpath, pointing right. Turn onto this path, walking through grass with a wall to your right.

The path climbs to join the track leading into Hollin Top farm. There is a gate across the track with a pedestrian gate beside it. Go through this and follow the track up to the farm. Go through another gate here and continue in the same direction; now on a rough tractor track with walls off to each side.

Walk up to the gate at the top of this lane. Beyond, the wall to the right heads off at a right-angle. Watch for a path leading off to the right, through bracken, and walk along with the wall to your right. When the wall bends to the right, go with it; passing through a pedestrian gate to enter a broad, grassy lane.

After 50m go through a gate in a fence, so that you now have a wall to your left and the fence to your right. Follow this path down to some stepping stones over a small stream. Beyond this, the clear path climbs to a pedestrian gate with a blue arrow on it. Go through this and walk up the left-hand side of a narrow field to a further gate, visible at the top of the field.

There is a house ahead of you. From the gate, the route, now marked by posts, swings off to the left (a deviation from the bridleway to avoid the house). The posts lead you to a point where you cross a stream. Beyond this the path – slabbed in places, faint in others – runs straight across heather moorland to reach the public road (if you lose the path, aim right rather than left to be sure to hit the road). There is no sign at the far end of the path, just a small cairn.

Turn left along the road (it can be busy, but the verges are clear). After 300m, just before the road crosses a stream, there is a sign for a bridleway pointing back-right. Turn on to this clear track and follow it across the moorland.

After half a mile/0.8km a wall comes in from the left and there are two junctions. First, the clear track bends off to the left, to run by the wall. Ignore this and keep straight on, on a rough footpath. A short way ahead, when the path reaches the curve of the wall, there is a three-way junction. Take the middle of the three tracks, going more or less straight on.

A clear track now descends quite steeply. Go through a gate in a wall and continue, now with a wall to your right and the houses of Danby visible below. Join a metalled road on the edge of the village. Turn left to reach the main road, then right to return to the start.

6 Danby to Commondale _____ A

A complex circuit linking two villages in Eskdale. The bulk of the walk is on clear tracks and a quiet public road, but some basic navigation is needed on one moorland stretch. Fine views of Eskdale. Length: **8 miles/13km**; *Height Climbed:* **390ft/120m** (on first climb; undulations thereafter).

O.S. Sheet OL26

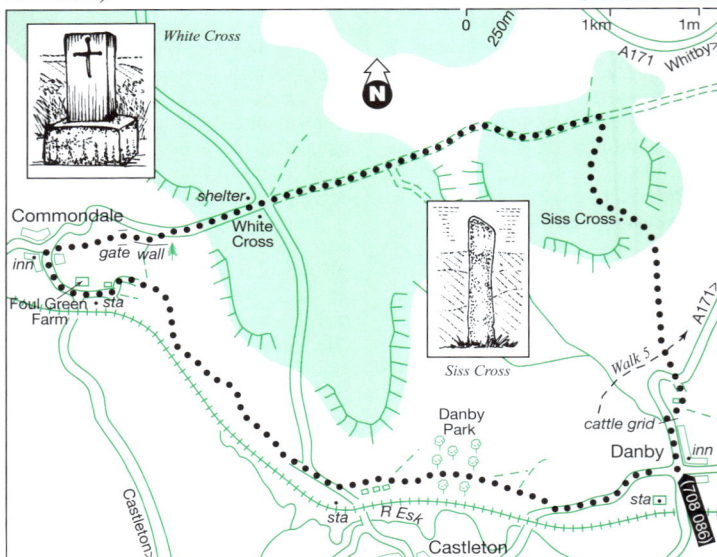

Danby is a small village in the upper Esk Valley. To reach it, drive west from Whitby on the A171 for about 12 miles then turn left (ie, south) on the road signposted for the village.

Park in the village and walk to the central crossroads, by the Duke of Wellington Inn. Take the north road (Scaling) and climb out of the village. The road crosses a cattle-grid; turn right immediately beyond at the sign for a footpath.

A rough track climbs towards a house. When it swings right, along the slope, keep straight on along a fainter path which leads to the right-hand side of the house. Join the driveway beyond the house and follow it to the public road.

Cross the road (carefully) to find a sign for a bridleway and walk straight on along a grassy path across the

7 Ingleby Bank   B

A fine circuit on good tracks, climbing to a moorland ridge then returning through farmland and woodland. Terrific views. Length:
5½ miles/8.8km; *Height Climbed:* **590ft/180m**. *Link with Walk 21.*

O.S. Sheet OL26

Ingleby Greenhow is a tiny village with an inn and a church, 3 miles south of Great Ayton on minor roads. Drive out of the centre on the road for Battersby and turn first right at the sign for Bank Foot. When you reach the first house a track cuts off to the right. Park to the left of this track, on the verge. (If there is no room, you will have to park back in the village and walk the first bit.)

Walk back to the junction and turn right, up through the houses to reach a gate. Go through this and follow the clear track beyond, winding up through the trees on Ingleby Bank and on to the open moor.

At the top of the bank the track swings hard right and a bridleway starts to the left. Ignore this and stick to the main track; climbing to the top of Tidy Brown Hill where the Cleveland Way joins from behind left. Continue along the main track for a further 1½ miles/2.6km, ignoring two paths heading off to the left, until you reach the highest point of the track.

If you look to the right at this point you will see another track running parallel. Look for a link path connecting the two tracks, walk across to the second track (the line of a disused railway) and turn right; descending the slope at a steady angle.

At the foot of the slope the track

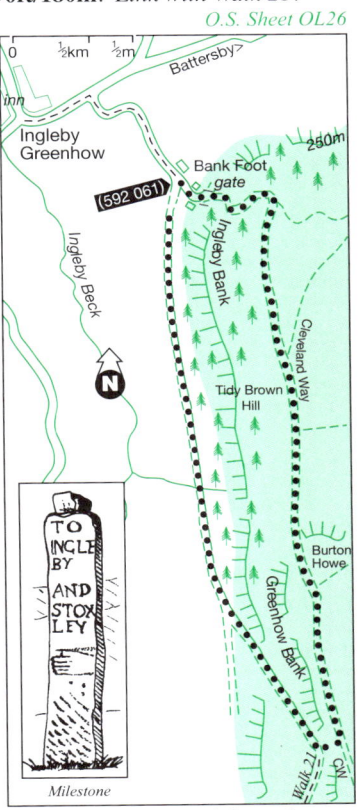

Milestone

edges to the right and follows the bottom of the wood back to the start of the walk.

moor. At this point some navigation will be necessary. The path is faint and there are other faint paths through the heather. When in doubt, remember that you are aiming to climb the low hill to the north (Siss Cross Hill). As you get nearer, you will see the post of Siss Cross on the horizon: the correct path passes the cross.

If you have lost the path, rejoin it at the Cross and continue across the moor. The path becomes clearer as it goes along: heading north in a wide curve around a marshy area before joining a clear track which runs across the moor. Turn left along the track.

The track runs clear for 1 1/2 miles/ 2.4km to the public road (one track cuts off to the left along the way: ignore it). You reach the road at a junction. Cross the road and continue in the same direction down the second road, with a bus shelter to your right and White Cross to your left.

The road runs straight for 1/2 mile/ 0.8km then curves to the right. When it does so, watch for a sign for a bridleway to the left, just after passing a clump of conifers. Turn onto a faint path which slowly converges with a wall to the left. As it nears the wall you will notice a wooden pedestrian gate in it: ignore this and continue with the wall to your left.

After a short distance the wall curves right and there is a gate in it (blue arrow). Go through this and walk down the slope below with a wall to your left, passing through two further gates on the way down to the village of Commondale. The Cleveland Inn is ahead of you.

Turn left (station). After a short distance you pass Foul Green Farm. The road swings right at this point (Castleton), but you go straight on (station, bridleway). The track for the station quickly cuts off to the right, but you keep straight on to pass to the right of a cottage, visible ahead. At the far end of the cottage a signposted path keeps straight on. Ignore this and follow the track round the end of the cottage and then on across the slope for 1 1/2 miles/2.4km to reach a junction with the public road.

Turn right down this road for 150m. Immediately beyond the village sign for Castleton turn left at a sign for a bridleway (Danby). Follow the clear track behind a line of houses. Beyond the last of them a path heads off ahead-left. Ignore this and continue, with a wall to your right.

Pass through a gate in a wall and continue with a fence to your right and a slope of bracken and birch to the left. When the fence ends you pass through another gate and continue through the woodland of Danby Park.

At the end of the wood you pass through a gate and continue with a wall to your right and moorland to the left. A path heads off to the left: ignore it.

You reach a post with blue arrows on it: one pointing left and the other straight on. Go straight on, sticking to the main path and ignoring paths to right and left to reach the public road. Turn left (take care, the road is narrow) to return to Danby.

The little village of Low Mill is in the heart of Farndale, about 6 miles north of Kirkbymoorside on minor roads. There is a car park in the village.

Walks 18 & 19) At the entrance to the car park there is a sign for a footpath to High Mill. Go through a gate and follow the clear path down to a footbridge over the River Dove then on up the riverside. This is a pleasant, well-maintained walk through fields and woodland.

After a little under 1½ miles/2.4km you reach the buildings at High Mill (including the Daffy Café). Walk a short distance on beyond the buildings until you see a sign to the left for a path to Cow Bank.

Walk 18) To reach the village of Church Houses, keep straight on along the metalled road. Return by the same route.

Walk 19) To continue with the longer circuit, go left here; crossing a stile then descending, over a marshy area, to reach a footbridge over the river, visible ahead.

From the far end of the bridge walk up the slope ahead, aiming for the top right-hand corner of the field. Cross a stile here then walk up the middle of the next field to reach the public road.

Turn right along the road. After a short distance you reach a junction. Go straight on (Dale End). Monket House is visible ahead, to the right of the road. Immediately beyond it a clear track heads left off the road (gate), marked by a sign for Bransdale.

Follow the track up to a gate in a wall then continue climbing up and across the slope. After a short distance a track cuts off to the left – ignore this: you will not be turning left until you reach the top of the ridge.

At the highest point there is a four-way junction. Go left, following the clear track along the ridge for ½ mile/0.8km until, a short distance after a sign for a bridleway to the left, you reach a second four-way junction. Go left here. (**NB:** if you are linking with Walk 20, keep straight on along the ridge.)

The track quickly becomes a path and continues running down and across the slope. At the point where a wall down to the left comes up to form a corner there is a split in the path, marked by a cairn. Keep right here. This leads you along the slope and then down to a gate in a wall.

Follow the arrows in the field to reach a stile/gate in the bottom left-hand corner of the field. Walk down the right-hand side of the field below to reach a bridge over West Gill Beck.

Cross the bridge and swing right, downstream. After a short distance you go through a gate, following a rough, damp track which runs to the left of the ruin at High Barn then continues down the valley.

Pass to the left of the buildings at Horn End and continue down the driveway to reach the public road. Turn right along the road for a short distance (it is narrow, so take care) to return to Low Mill.

20 Rudland Rigg ⎯⎯⎯⎯⎯⎯⎯⎯⎯⎯⎯⎯⎯⎯⎯⎯⎯ A

A fine high loop through farmland and moorland. Good paths; excellent views over Farndale. Length: **7 miles/11.2km**; *Height Climbed:* **820ft/250m**. *Possible link with Walk 19.*

O.S. Sheet OL26

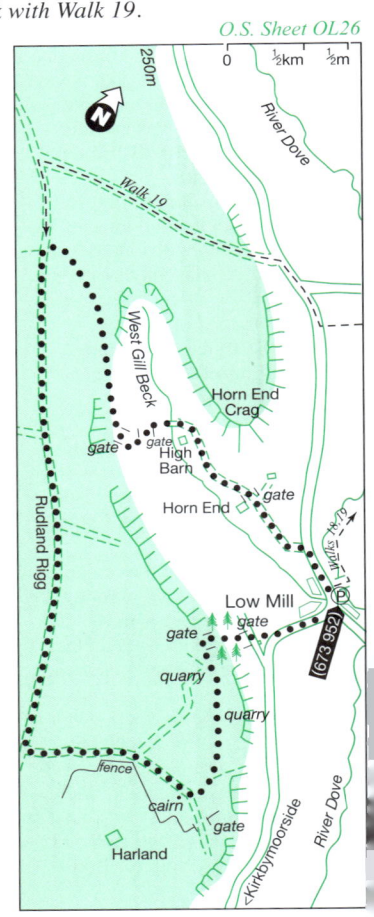

The little village of Low Mill is in the heart of Farndale, about 6 miles north of Kirkbymoorside on minor roads. There is a car park in the village.

Walk out of the car park and turn right, up the narrow road. After a short distance a signposted track opens up to the left (bridleway, Rudland Rigg). Follow the track to the pantiled farm at Horn End.

Pass to the right of the farm buildings. A track cuts off to the right at this point. Ignore this: pass through a gate with an arrow on it and follow the clear track up the valley.

The track passes to the right of the ruin at High Barn. Just beyond there are two gates, one after the other. Cross a stile by the first but do not go through the other: head slightly left, so you are walking with a wall to your right. Pass through another gate just beyond then swing left to cross a footbridge over West Gill Beck.

Climb up the left-hand side of the field beyond the bridge to reach a stile/gate in a stone wall. Beyond this a grassy track winds up the last field to reach a gate in the top right-hand corner. Follow the rough path beyond, running up and across the slope, through grass at first and then heather, to reach a junction with a clear track at the top of the ridge.

Turn left along the track and follow it for 2 miles/3.2km, until you are almost level with the first walled fields starting off to your left. At this point a track heads off left (no sign). Turn on to this and continue, eventually joining a fence to your right. (**NB:** This path is not a right of way and may be closed for brief periods.)

Another track heads off to the left. Ignore this and keep turning right. Continue until you can see a gate in a fence ahead, then start watching for a small cairn to the right of the track. This marks the right of way. Turn onto a faint path heading back-left.

The path splits. Take the left-hand path, which ends up running along the top of the ridge above Farndale. This is a pleasant path, with fine views, passing two old quarries. In the second, larger, quarry the path splits. Keep right.

The path now descends, across the slope, to reach a conifer wood. Go through a gate and follow a track through the wood. Go through another gate at the foot of the wood then head half-right down a field to reach a gate leading onto the public road.

Cross the road and follow a signposted path down the left-hand side of a house. Go straight downhill beyond, through two fields and a garden, to reach the public road. Turn left to return to the start.

21 Head of Farndale _____ A/B/C

A level, lineal route along an old railway line, through moorland above Farndale. Length: up to 7½ miles/12km (one way, to link with Walks 7 & 19); Height Climbed: none.

O.S. Sheet OL26

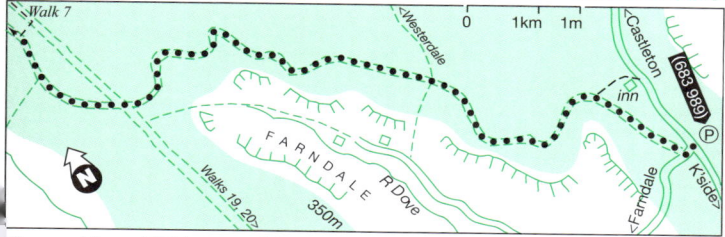

The road from Kirkbymoorside north to Castleton runs along Blakey Ridge. Five miles north of Hutton-le-Hole (½ mile south of the Lion Inn) a road cuts west into Farndale. There is a car park opposite the road end.

Walk a few steps down the Farndale road then turn right at the sign for a bridleway. A clear track runs off ahead – the bed of an old industrial railway, contouring around the head of the dale. It takes a long time to get anywhere, but the views are terrific. Walk as far as you wish then return – possibly *via* the Lion Inn (*see* map).

Ambitious walkers will find links between this walk and Walks 7, 19 and 20.

22 Hutton-le-Hole — B

A lineal walk over open moorland on good tracks, with a possible return by a quiet public road. Fine views. **Length: 5 miles/8km**; *Height Climbed:* **560ft/170m**. *Possible link with Walks 23, 24.*

O.S. Sheet OL26

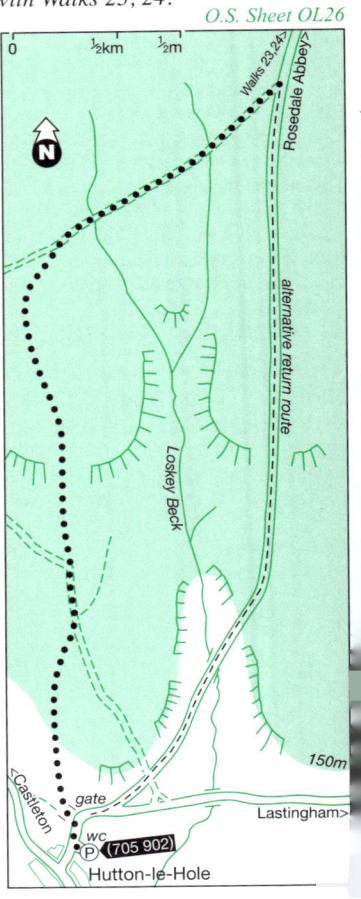

Hutton-le-Hole is a picturesque village 3 miles north of Kirkbymoorside along minor roads. It is the home of the Rydale Folk Museum.

Park in the car park at the northern end of the village. Walk out of the car park and turn right, up the road. The road quickly begins to turn right. As it does so, look for a path to the left, leading to a wooden pedestrian gate.

Beyond the gate the path immediately splits. Keep right, on a slightly sunken, grassy path. After ¹/₂ mile/0.8km the path joins a tarmac road. A sign on a rock points left for the footpath. After 400m a grassy path starts to the right, marked by an arrow on a rusty metal post. Turn on to this path.

After a further ³/₄ mile/1.2km the path reaches a high point and swings right. After a short distance it joins a clear track coming in from behind-left. Turn right along this and continue: crossing two becks before climbing to join the public road.

Here you have a choice. You can return by the same route or, if you wish a different view, turn right along the road (it is unfenced and has wide verges, but you might choose to avoid it if it is busy). If you wish to extend your walk, turn left along the road for ¹/₂ mile/0.8km to reach Walks 23 and 24. The former passes Ana Cross – visible on the horizon ahead.

23 Ana Cross & Rosedale — B

A moderate circuit on good tracks, ending with a steep climb on the public road. Through moorland and farmland, and passing an imposing landmark. Length: **4 miles/6.4km**; *Height Climbed:* **525ft/160m**. *Link with Walk 24.*

The village of Rosedale Abbey is in the heart of Rosedale: 7 miles north of Kirkbymoorside on minor roads. Ana Cross is a large stone cross on a hill to the south of the village. For the walk to the cross, park in the car park by the road south to Hutton-le-Hole, 1/2 mile south of Rosedale Abbey at the top of a Rosedale Bank.

Cross the road from the car park and walk along the clear track heading towards the cross. Just before the cross the track splits. Go left.

After a further 1/4 mile/0.4km you reach a four-way junction. Keep straight on. Once the track has swung round to the left start looking for a path to the left, marked by a very small cairn. Turn on to this path (if you find yourself passing a quarry, you have missed the turn).

The path runs on over the moorland, gradually swinging to the left to run along the edge above the valley. A clear path comes in from behind-right: ignore this and follow the rough path down and across the slope to join the wall above Hollins Farm.

Go left along the wall to join the track leading into the farm then follow this track along the slope, passing through a number of gates along the way, to join the public road just beyond the White Horse Farm Hotel.

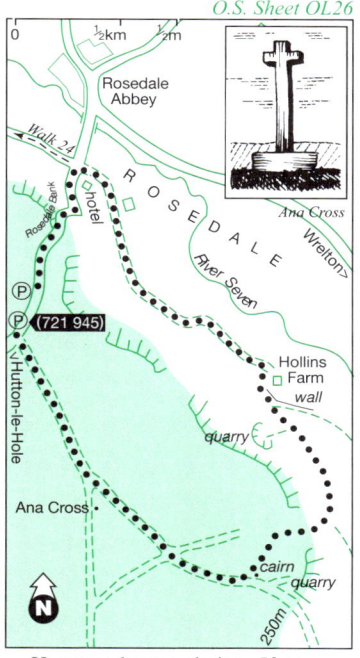

O.S. Sheet OL26

Here you have a choice. If you wish to link with Walk 24, keep straight on along the road opposite to Thorgill; otherwise turn left, climbing the steep road as it zig-zags up Rosedale Bank (be careful to keep out of the way of traffic), to return to the start.

24 Thorgill ─────────────────────────────── B

A circuit which starts along a quiet road and returns by an old railway line through the moorland, with a steep, damp hill climb in between.
Length: **5 miles/8km**; *Height Climbed:* **525ft/160m**. *Link with Walk 23.*

O.S. Sheet OL26

To reach the start of this walk, follow the instructions for Walk 23. Instead of parking at the top car park, however, use the next one down the bank.

Walk out of the car park and turn left, downhill on the public road (take care on this stretch and keep out of the way of traffic). At the foot of the slope, opposite the White Horse Farm Hotel, turn left onto the road for Thorgill.

Follow this narrow, quiet public road up the dale for 1¼ miles/2km, until you reach the edge of the little village of Thorgill. A sign points left for a footpath to Farndale. Walk up to a junction with a road leading past a line of cottages. Turn left to reach a pedestrian gate at the top of the road.

Edge right beyond the gate. The ground is broken and damp in this section, so you may wish to climb the slope a little then walk along parallel to the walls down to your right.

When the fields end to the right you drop down to cross a moss-covered bridge over a beck, just above the last wall. Beyond this a faint path climbs straight up the slope ahead to join the line of the old railway by the single gable-end and fenced off pit (keep away from this, it is dangerous) of Sheriff's Pit.

Turn left along the old railway, which contours along the edge of the dale for a little over 1½ miles/2.6km. When a row of cottages appears a little way down the slope, take the path which descends to join the track behind them. (If you wish to link with Walk 23, just continue along the main track.) Follow this past the old kilns of the Rosedale Iron Works and back to the car park.

9 Round Hill _____A

A moderate climb across moorland to the highest point in the North York Moors, with a return along clear tracks and rough paths. Length:
5½ miles/9km; *Height Climbed:* **720ft/220m**.

O.S. Sheet OL26

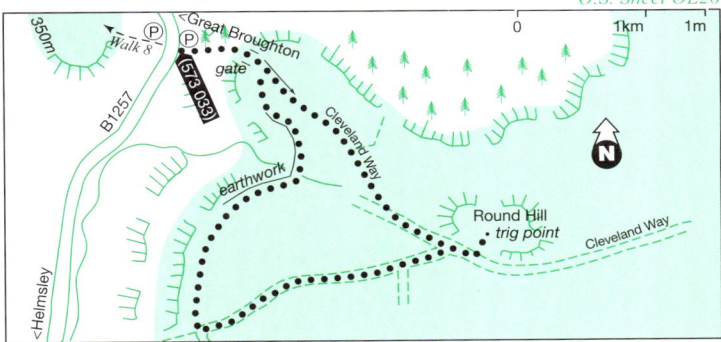

Start this walk from Clay Bank car park, at the highest point of the B1257, 2 miles south of the village of Great Broughton.

There are car parks to either side of the road, and at the southern end of the parking areas there are signs pointing east and west. Take the east path (sign: Cleveland Way, Bloworth Crossing).

Climb a steep path – initially with a plantation to your left – to reach a pedestrian gate in a wall. Go through and continue, with a wall still to the left. After 20m you reach a signposted junction. Keep straight on (the path to the right is the return route).

After a little over ½ mile/1km a bridleway heads off to the left. Stick to the main track. When you join a clearer track, coming in from behind-right and heading off ahead-left, go left. At the next junction (a clear track coming in from behind-right – your return route) keep straight on for a short distance to reach the undistinguished peak of Round Hill, marked by a trig point.

After enjoying the view, retrace your steps to the last junction and go left (no sign). After a short distance a track heads off to the left. Ignore this and continue until the track turns sharp left at the edge of the moor.

Turn right here, off the track. There is a rough path, but it disappears in places. If in doubt, just keep straight on. Ultimately you will be dropping to the left to join a path along the old earthwork on the edge of the moor. This zig-zags right then left to cross a small stream, then runs on, clearer now, to rejoin the original path.

8 The Wain Stones _____B

A short loop starting through grazing land then returning along an open ridge via a fine tor. Excellent views. Length: **3 miles/5km**; *Height Climbed:* **490ft/150m**.

O.S. Sheet OL26

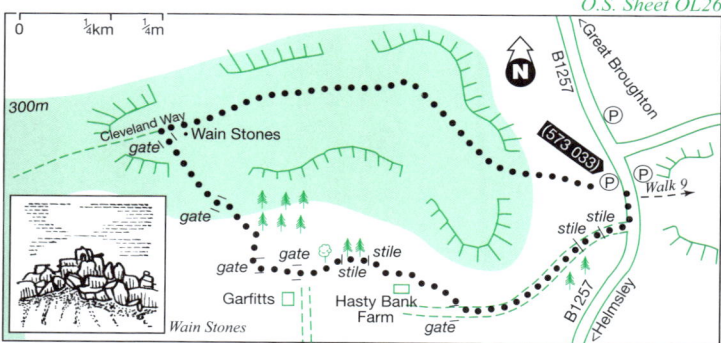

To reach the start of this walk, follow the directions for Walk 9. Walk to the south end of the car park. A sign for the Cleveland Way points up some steps to the right (west). That is the return path. To start the walk go just beyond this and turn right onto a driveway.

Follow this drive, crossing stiles beside two gates. At the third gate a yellow arrow points ahead-right. Go that way, with a wall (later a fence) to your left and a bank up to the right.

Follow the fence round Hasty Bank Farm until a fence blocks your way and there is a stile to your left. Cross that (arrow), now going downhill with a wall to your right. At the end of a block of conifers to your right there is a stile. Cross that, now passing through scrub woodland.

The path crosses a small stream and a marshy area (duckboards) then swings left towards the buildings at Garfitts. As you approach the buildings a sign points right to a pedestrian gate. Go through this and walk on with a fence to your right to reach a farm gate in a wall. Go through this and turn right on a rough track, climbing with a wall to your right.

When the track reaches the bottom corner of a conifer plantation it veers left, aiming for the Wain Stones on the horizon. It reaches a fence and swings left along it to reach a gate in a wall. Beyond this it climbs to a gate in a wall almost on the ridge.

Go through this and turn immediately right to pass through a gap in a wall. The path is now quite clear, climbing to the broken rocks then continuing along the ridge before dropping back down to the road.

10 Newgate Bank ──────────────────────────── B

A pleasant walk on good paths; out through conifer woodland and back along the edge of a moor. Good views. Length: **5 miles/8km**; *Height Climbed:* **460ft/140m**.

O.S. Sheet OL26

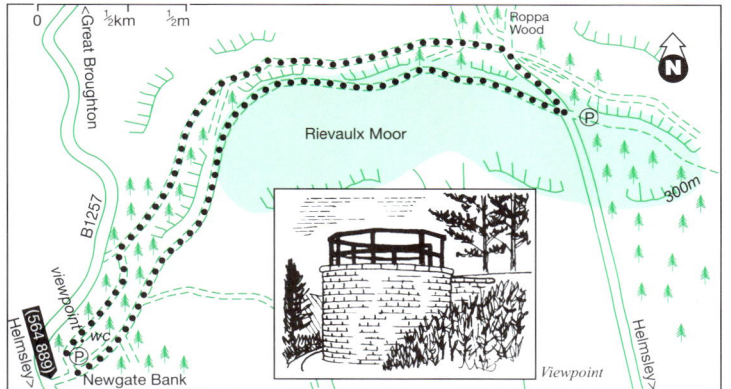

Viewpoint

The Newgate Bank car park is at the south end of Bilsdale, just where it joins Ryedale. To reach it, drive 4½ miles north from Helmsley on the B1257. The car park is to the right (east) of the road.

It is a large car park. Near the start of it you will see a sign for a bridleway, pointing left. Follow the path for ½ mile/0.8km, eventually swinging left and descending to a signposted T-junction with a track. Turn right (bridleway).

You follow this track through trees at first, then with trees to the right and fields down to the left. A track comes in from behind-right. Ignore it and keep straight on.

The fields become moorland and a line of trees is visible ahead (Roppa Wood). As you enter the wood a second track joins from behind-right. Keep straight on to reach a complex junction of tracks (some signed). Turn right here (no sign), climbing up and across the wooded slope on a track which becomes a tarmac road.

At the top of the climb you reach the edge of the Rievaulx Moor, with a car park to the left and signed paths starting to right and left. Go right, following a clear, rough track with an old fence to the right and the open moor to the left.

After 2 miles/3.2km of moorland the track runs back into the trees. Within about 100m the track splits. Keep right here and follow the clear track back down to the entrance to the car park.

Walks North York Moors: West

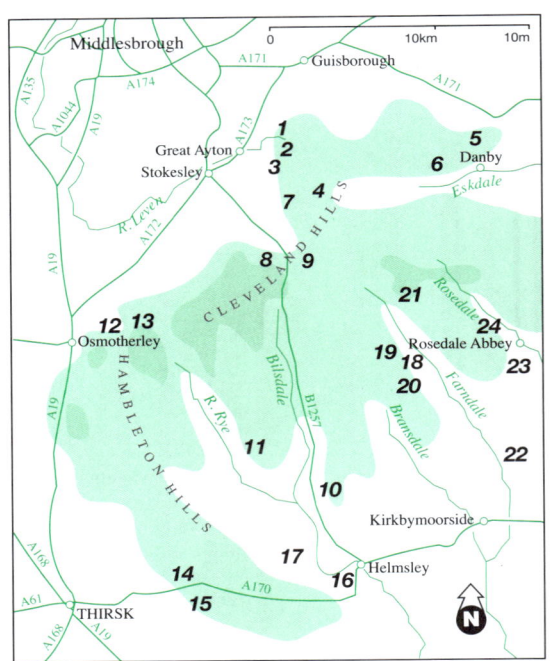

Grades

A ...... Full walking equipment required

B ...... Strong walking footwear and waterproof clothing required

C ...... Comfortable walking footwear recommended

NB: Assume each walk increases at least one grade in winter conditions. Hill routes can become treacherous.

Walks North York Moors: West

	walk	grade
1	Roseberry Topping	B
2	Great Ayton Moor	B
3	Cook Monument	B
4	Baysdale	B
5	Danby	B
6	Danby to Commondale	A
7	Ingleby Bank	B
8	The Wain Stones	B
9	Round Hill	A
10	Newgate Bank	B
11	Hawnby Moor	A
12	Cod Beck Reservoir	C
13	Osmotherley Loop	B
14	Sutton Bank & Gormire Lake	B
15	White Horse Trail	B
16	Helmsley to Rievaulx	B
17	Rievaulx	B
18	Low Mill to Church Houses	C
19	West Farndale	A
20	Rudland Rigg	A
21	Head of Farndale	A/B/C
22	Hutton-le-Hole	B
23	Ana Cross & Rosedale	B
24	Thorgill	B

— www.pocketwalks.com —

Published by: *Hallewell Publications, Scotland*
Printed by: *Barr Printers, Glenrothes*

While every care has been taken in the preparation of this guide, the publishers cannot accept responsibility for any loss, damage or injury resulting from its use.

11 **Hawnby Moor** _____ A

A complex circuit over moorland and through farmland, visiting the little village of Fangdale Beck. The paths are faint in places and some care will need to be taken with navigation. Length: **7½ miles/12km**; *Total Height Climbed:* **1,120ft/340m**.

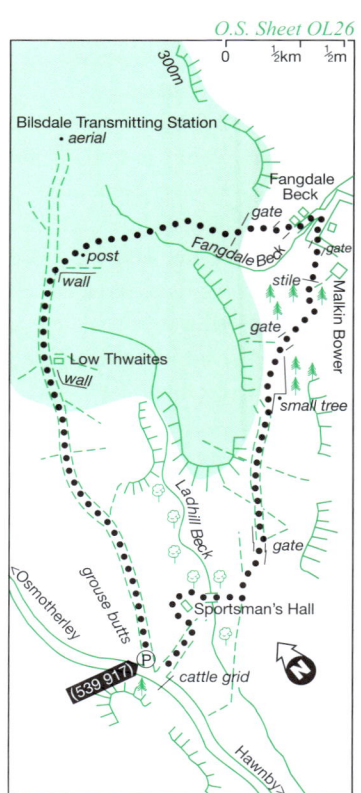

The tiny village of Hawnby is in Ryedale, surrounded by the hills and moors in the south-west corner of the North York Moors. To reach it, drive north from Helmsley (13 miles east of Thirsk on the A170) on the B1257 road for Great Broughton. Follow this road for 3½ miles then turn left onto a minor road and follow the signs for Hawnby.

From the village, take the road signed for Osmotherley. Follow this for a little over a mile to reach the high point of the road. Just beyond a cattle grid there is a small conifer wood to the left and a parking area to the right. Park here.

There is a sign for a footpath pointing through the car park but for this walk take the clear track signed as 'unsuitable for motor vehicles', with the tall aerial of Bilsdale Transmitting Station visible ahead.

After a mile/1.6km the clear track splits. Keep left here (no sign). After a further ¾ mile/1.2km the track joins a wall to the right, passes the ruin at Low Thwaites, then continues for a further ½ mile/0.8km until the wall bends sharply away to the right.

At this point there is a junction, with a clear track continuing to the Transmitting Station and another going right, by the wall. Look ahead-right at this point for a stone post visible on the horizon. Walk towards this through the heather (you may stumble upon a path).

The small path passes directly to the left of the post then continues towards a concrete post, then on to another, and so on until it reaches Fangdale Beck. Cross this. Beyond, the path, marshy in places but always fairly obvious, climbs to the top of the bank and swings right down the top of the ridge. There are no more posts but you will see the occasional pile of stones.

Descend and go through the line of an old wall, then continue straight ahead, through bracken, with the line of an old wall off to the right. The path then becomes clearer (it may be damp in this section) and passes through two pedestrian gates in old walls before reaching a gate on the edge of Fangdale Beck with a blue arrow on it, pointing right.

Walk a short distance between walls, pass between two houses then swing left on a gavel drive. Go through the house gate to join the public road and follow this down through the hamlet with the beck to your right.

At the end of the houses there is a junction. Go right, back up past the houses. Just above the village the road bends hard left and heads towards a farm (Malkin Bower). As you approach the farm there is a pedestrian gate to the right and a sign for a footpath. Turn right here and walk up through two fields with a wall to your right. At the top of the second field there is a stile, beyond which you scramble up a steep slope to join a track. Turn right up this.

The track goes through a gate then winds off to the left, by a wall. Ignore a field entrance to the left and continue climbing to reach a gate in a wall on the edge of the moor.

Beyond this the track splits. Keep left, by the wall at first. As you approach a stand of conifers the path swings right and climbs, running roughly parallel to them. There are a number of paths and tracks in this area. Look ahead and you will see the top corner of the field walls with a small tree growing from it. Aim for that.

Beyond the field corner continue with the wall to your left. After a short distance you join a clear track coming in from behind-right. Follow this by the wall for a further 1/2 mile/0.8km to reach a four-way junction with a wall to your left. Go straight ahead here, on a clear track which now begins to peel away from the wall to the left.

The track recrosses the moor. Half way across there is a four-way junction. Keep straight on to reach a gate in a step in the wall on the far side. Go through this. The path runs by the wall for a short distance then edges down the slope to the right. Almost level with Sportsman's Hall (on the far side of the valley), an arrow points right.

Follow a rough path straight downhill to reach a gap in a fence, then edge to the right to reach a footbridge over the beck. Beyond this, follow a sequence of arrows through the fields around the farm to join a track just by the farm entrance. Turn right here to return to the start.

12 **Cod Beck Reservoir** / 13 **Osmotherley Loop** _C/B_

12) *A short walk on flat paths through woodland around a small reservoir. Length:* **1½ miles/2.5km***; Height Climbed:* none. **13)** *A complex loop through woodland and farmland and over the open moor. The paths are generally good and there are fine views – plus a visit to the picturesque village of Osmotherley. Length:* **5½ miles/8.8km***; Total Height Climbed:* **625ft/190m***.*

O.S. Sheet OL26

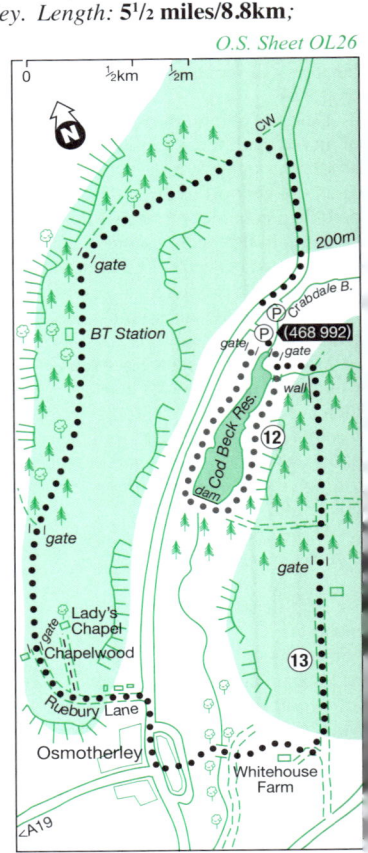

Osmotherley is a pleasant little village to the east of the A19, just south of its junction with the A172. Drive up to the junction in the centre of Osmotherley and turn north (sign: Cote Ghyll Caravan Park). Follow this road for 1 mile to reach the little car park, to the right of the road, at the far end of Cod Beck Reservoir. (If this is full, there is a second, larger car park a little further along the road.)

Walks 12 & 13) Walk out of the back of the car park and cross little Crabdale Beck just beyond (stepping stones). Walk on to the metal kissing-gate which leads into the conifer forest. Beyond this, climb the set of wooden-fronted steps at the start of the reservoir path.

After a short distance you reach a small beck crossed by a concrete bridge.

Walk 12) Cross the bridge and follow the clear track to the end of the reservoir. Turn right, across the dam, then follow the path through the woodland on the far side of the reservoir back to the car park.

Walk 13) Turn left on the near side of the beck. The path climbs through the trees, becoming clearer as it does so. After a short climb the path swings right, over the beck, and continues across the slope with a broken-down wall to the right.

Continue straight through the wood. A clear track comes in from the left and runs on ahead. Follow this until it bends away to the right, at which point you keep straight on along a fainter path.

At the end of the wood you pass through two gates then continue across the slope with a wall to the right. Follow this track for 3/4 mile/1.2km. Once it has begun to descend watch for a sign pointing right, through a gap in a wall, for the Cleveland Way (CW).

Just beyond the wall, join a track leading towards a house. Shortly before the house is reached a second CW sign points right. The path crosses the corner of a field then descends the slope, passing through two gates on the way, to reach a track running across the bottom of the slope.

Walk directly across the track and into the trees beyond to reach a footbridge over a beck. Climb the slope beyond then follow the fenced lane into Osmotherley. Cross the first road you meet and walk down a lane through the houses to reach the main street through the village. Turn right.

Once you are beyond the edge of the village watch for a sign pointing left for the CW, up Ruebury Lane. Follow this past a string of houses and then on through farmland. When the lane begins to bend to the right there is a fork. A brief diversion to the right leads to Lady's Chapel (open to the public), but for this walk keep left and follow the track to Chapelwood farm.

Pass to the right of the farm buildings and you reach three gates leading into a field. Go through the middle (pedestrian) gate then follow the track to the left, along the bottom of the field.

Keep straight on until you reach a gate on the edge of a wood. Beyond the gate the track splits. Go right, on a track which climbs to the top of the wood then continues with a fence to the right and fields beyond that.

Pass to the right of a BT station and continue to reach a gate/stile leading onto an area of open moorland (CW). The path beyond leads across the moorland, pulling away from the wall to the left.

A little further on the path rejoins the wall then swings to the right. There is a signposted junction. The CW goes left, but for this route go ahead-right (bridleway). Follow this down to the public road then turn right to return to the start.

Lady's Chapel

14 Sutton Bank & Gormire Lake_____B

A short but steep walk: descending through fine woodland to a small lake, climbing back then returning along the cliff top. Terrific views.
Length: **2½ miles/4km**; *Height Climbed:* **460ft/140m**.

O.S. Sheet OL26

Start from the car park at Sutton Bank, by the National Park Information Centre: 5 miles east of Thirsk on the A170.

From the car park, follow the A170 to the point where it swings left to descend Sutton Bank. At this point you have to cross a minor road to reach a sign for the Cleveland Way (Sneck Yate). Follow the clear path beyond along the top of the bank.

After a short distance the lake becomes visible below and you reach a signposted junction. Go left here (nature trail), following a rough, steep path down and across the slope through Garbutt Wood.

Pass to the right of a large boulder then follow the path down through more woodland to reach a signposted split. Go left here (Gormire Lake). This leads down to the path by the side of the lake. Turn right.

Walk along the side of the lake and continue on the clear path beyond. After a short distance you reach a signposted three-way junction of bridleways. Go back-right (if you reach Southwoods Lodge you have gone too far).

The path zig-zags up through the wood, sunken and wet in places. You start by climbing across the slope to the right, then double back, almost across the slope, to reach an old quarry. Cut back to the right here, then back to the left to climb to the top of the wood, with an old wall to your left and a low cliff directly ahead.

The path swings left and climbs to the path above the cliff (the Cleveland Way). If you wish to extend your walk, it is possible to turn left and continue along the top of the brow. For this route, turn right and return to the start along the cliff top.

15 White Horse Trail _____B

A moderate loop, with some steep climbing, along the top of fine cliffs then through woodland to reach the figure of a white horse on the hillside. Length: **3 miles/5km**; *Height Climbed:* **300ft/90m**.

Start from the car park at Sutton Bank, by the National Park Information Centre: 5 miles east of Thirsk on the A170.

Walk to the far west corner of the car park, cross the A170 (carefully), just before it drops over the edge of the bank, and join the clear path on the far side (sign: White Horse).

The path follows the top of the bank, and the cliffs of Roulston Scar soon appear ahead. Continue along the bank for ¾ mile/1km, keeping an eye open for low-flying gliders, until you reach an information board carrying information about the gliding strip to your left. At this point head right (white arrow) on a path with a wooden fence to the right, dropping down and across the wooded slope.

After the initial descent a path comes in from behind-right. Keep left (white arrow) and follow the path beneath Roulston Scar. When it splits follow the clearer, left-hand path, which now begins to climb.

A track comes in from behind-right. Ignore this and continue to a small car park – the white horse should now be visible up to your left. Walk straight across the car park. Before you reach the far entrance turn left (White Horse Walk) and climb the steps to the right of the horse.

The horse – about 320ft/100m long – was completed in 1857 and is best

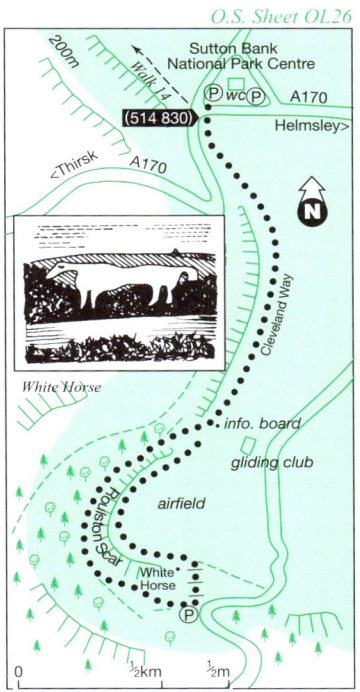

viewed from the village of Kilburn, to the south. You are asked not to walk on the figure itself.

The path swings left along the top of the horse then rejoins the Cleveland Way. Follow this back along the cliff top, with the gliding club to your right, to return to the start.

16 Helmsley to Rievaulx _____ B

A lineal route, following part of the Cleveland Way, linking the picturesque village of Helmsley, with its fine old castle, with the ruined abbey at Rievaulx. Possible link with Walk 17. Length: **3½ miles/5.5km** *(one way); Height Climbed:* **295ft/90m**.

O.S. Sheet OL26

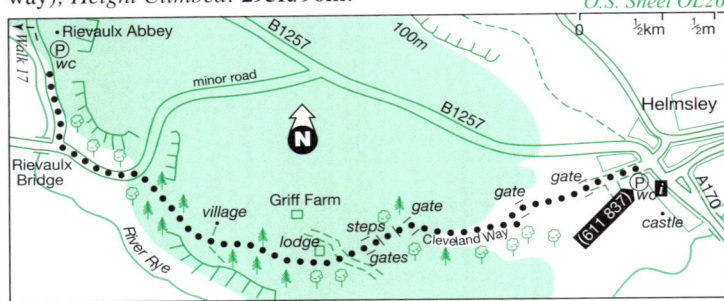

Helmsley is a handsome village 13 miles east of Thirsk on the A170, famous for its ruined 12th/13th-century castle. Park in the long stay car park at the west end of the village. Walk back to the entrance, just beyond the toilets, and turn left (sign: Cleveland Way, Rievaulx). You are on a clear track. When a track cuts off to the left (Helmsley Walled Garden) keep straight on.

The path follows a lane for a short way, then passes through a gate and continues straight ahead along the left-hand edge of two grazing fields. At the end of the second field pass through a kissing gate and turn hard left, between a hedge and a fence.

At the bottom of the lane turn right, now with a wall to your left and trees beyond that. Go through a kissing gate. The wall to the left ends and you edge to the left, down into the trees, quickly joining a flight of stone steps. Cross a low point in the wood then climb more steps beyond.

Pass through two gates at the top of the wood then continue on a clear path with trees to your left. You approach a lodge house: cross a driveway then pass to the left of the lodge on a clear path (Cleveland Way).

The path begins to drop across the slope through conifer woodland. A track crosses the way from behind-left to ahead-right. A short detour to the right at this point leads to the grassy mounds which are all that remain of a deserted medieval village. Otherwise continue, descending through pleasant woodland to reach the public road.

In order to reach Rievaulx – a further mile/1.6km from this point – turn left down this road, then right at the junction on the near side of Rievaulx Bridge.

17 Rievaulx ─────────────────────────────────── B

A moderate circuit, through farmland and woodland and along quiet public roads, offering fine views of a splendid ruined abbey. Length:
4 miles/6.5km; *Total Height Climbed:* **260ft/80m**.

O.S. Sheet OL26

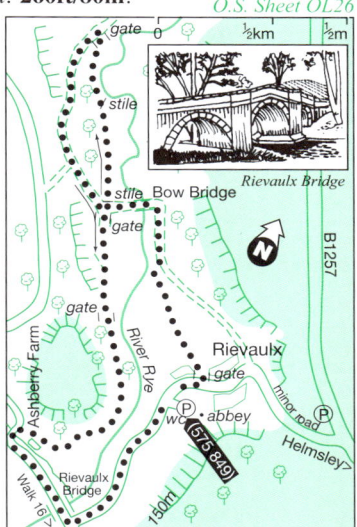

The village of Rievaulx is 2 miles north-west of Helmsley on the B1257 and a minor road. (Alternatively, it can be reached by following Walk 16.) There is a car park for the Abbey in the village. If you are visiting the splendid ruins then you can park here for the walk. If you are not then this can be expensive. If you are prepared to walk a little further there is a free parking area by the B1257 (*see* map).

Starting from the Abbey car park, walk into the village. Turn left at the sign for a path to Bow Bridge. Go through a gate, passing a stable. Cross a stream, go through a gate and cross a narrow field before veering left, with a hedge to your right, to reach a gate in the corner of the field.

Keep straight on beyond this to reach the river, then turn right (arrow) to join a track. Turn left along this and follow it over the hump-backed Bow Bridge. Beyond this the track runs straight for a short distance then swings to the left. Here there is a gate/stile to the right (sign: Hawnby). Cross the stile and follow a rough path at the foot of a wooded slope.

The path rejoins the River Rye. Go left, across a stile, and follow the path through the trees by the river. When the river bends away the path leaves the trees and keeps straight on to reach a gate leading onto a metalled road. Turn left along this.

When the track forks keep left. Just short of the junction previously passed there is a gate to the right and a sign for Ashberry. Go through the gate and follow a grassy path for a short distance to reach a gate on the edge of Ashberry Wood. Beyond this a clear path leads around the hill to join the public road at Ashberry Farm.

Turn left, crossing a bridge over a stream, then left again immediately (be careful, the roads are narrow). Follow the road over Rievaulx Bridge and turn left at the junction beyond to return to the start.

18 Low Mill to Church Houses /
19 West Farndale ——————————————— C/A

18) *A short, lineal walk, on a path through fields and woodland by a river, leading to a tea room and an inn (may be busy in daffodil season). Length:* **1¾ miles/2.8km** *(one way); Height Climbed:* **negligible**.
19) *A high-level extension of Walk 18, returning via the high moors. Good paths and excellent views. Length:* **6½ miles/10.4km***; Height Climbed:* **820ft/250m***. Possible link with Walk 20.*

O.S. Sheet OL26